NORTHBOUND

NORTHBOUND

Poems Selected and New

LEONA GOM

Thistledown Press

Copyright © Leona Gom, 1984

Canadian Cataloguing in Publication Data
  Gom, Leona, 1946 -
    NorthBound

      ISBN 0-920066-80-1 (bound). — ISBN 0-920066-77-1 (pbk.)

      I. Title.
      PS8563.04N6 1984   C811'.54   C84-091084-3
      PR9199.3.G65N6 1984

Book design by A.M. Forrie
Cover design/illustration by Carling Wong

Typesetting by Apex Design Graphics Ltd., Saskatoon
Set in 11 point Century

Printed and bound in Canada by
Hignell Printing Limited, Winnipeg

Thistledown Press
668 East Place
Saskatoon, Sask.
S7J 2Z5

Acknowledgements

Part I of ths book consists of selected poems from *Kindling* (Fiddlehead Press, 1972) and from *The Singletree* (Sono Nis Press, 1975). Part II consists of selected poems from *Land of the Peace* (Thistledown Press, 1980). All three of these books are now out of print. Part III consists of new poems which have not previously appeared in book form.

The author's work has appeared in the following periodicals: *Dalhousie Review, West Coast Review, Canadian Forum, Malahat Review, Queen's Quarterly, Miss Chatelaine, Salt, Waves, White Pelican, Grain, Other Voices, Northern Journey, Repository, The Whole Apple, Branching Out, Sunbury 10: New York, Poetry Canada Review, Room of One's Own, Nebula, Matrix, Arc, Ariel, Descant, Antigonish Review, Dandelion, Origins, Writing*

and in the following anthologies: *Forty Women Poets of Canada, 39 Below, Women's Eye, Canadian Humour and Satire, End of the World Speshul, New: West Coast, Western Moods, D'Sonoqua, Going for Coffee, Alberta Diamond Jubilee Anthology, Writing Right: New Poetry by Canadian Women, Ride Off Any Horizon, From Dustbowl to Peace River, The Maple Laugh Forever, Femme Plurielle* (in translation), *Anthology of Magazine Verse and Yearbook of American Poetry*

Her work has also been broadcast on CBC, CKUA Edmonton and CFRO Vancouver.

This book has been published with the assistance of the Saskatchewan Arts Board and The Canada Council.

Contents

New Poems

from *Kindling* (1972) and
The Singletree (1975)

The Singletree

The air like glass,
      I remember,
and thinking the breaths of the horses
    were fogging it up
as my own breath
    whitened the window
where I watched my father
    harnessing the team,
and one of them suddenly,
why I could not see,
      kicked violently
      at the lifted singletree,
and it cracked
    and fell from my father's hands,
and he stood very still,
    looking at it,
even when the horse was calm again,
he only stood there,
    looking at it,
    heavy in the snow,
and I may have wanted to cry,
and his breath bled white and vanishing
    around the shards of air,
    across the backs of the horses.

Justice

I always had this craving for salt
but mother had a horror
about my getting "high blood pressure"
or something so she'd put
all the salt shakers
up too high for me to reach,
but I outsmarted her
by squatting out in the pasture
for hours at a time
and licking blissfully
the big red salt block
that a cow would usually share
with me on the other side,
but mother caught me at it one day
and she paddled my bottom
right there in front of the cow
who watched in placid amusement,
so I really grew to hate cows
who could lick all the salt they wanted
and never get a licking.
Now of course I'm old enough
to see it's wrong to hate
those poor dumb animals
and I really pity them instead
because they all probably die
of high blood pressure.

Ode to the Outhouse

In summer, an idyllic place,
a place to meditate,
a refuge for the anti-social;
only cats and squirrels would wander in
to check how animate you were.
Idyllic.
Winter, that was something else.
Bladders would expand capacity fantastically,
and constipation was a consummation
devoutly to be wished.
(One Christmas, 45 below two weeks,
I swear I never had to go, not once,
my body understandingly recycling
all my wastes.)
But then, the body could rebel,
and cause a desperate midnight rush,
buttocks cringing at the icy seat
which acted like an enema.
Bowel and bladder would respond
at quite explosive speeds.
When our farm got electricity,
my father proudly hung a heat lamp
just above the seat.
This was a dubious improvement.
One would have to perch
at just the proper angle,
or one hemisphere got frostbite
while the other burned.
The best solution, still, was continence.
There are nostalgic contrasts to be made
between our pristine, soulless bathrooms
and those outhouses of old,
but nothing can, for me, compete
with toilets thermostatically controlled.

Hilda

Watching him go mad,
closing in on himself
like the land closed in,
snuffing his crops and his sanity
with 8-month winters
and arid summers
and isolation.
Was that the worst,
the isolation?
That what drove him
to meet his friends
in the yard with a rifle,
drove him finally
to fire at police,
your son helping him,
harvesting at last
his citizenship
from this brutal country,
a bullet in the brain?
And when you heard,
heard he had not died,
did you think
what the town thought,
the town that relished
the scandal he was,
that said it would be better
if he'd died?
Perhaps by then
you were gone,
no one knows where,
the land behind you
closing like a fist.

The First Album

   It belongs really to the horses,
on every page, patient in harness,
hitched to plows, hayracks, stoneboats, binders,
framed in collars and blinders,
the teams, singletrees heavy between them,
ponderous Clydesdale feet solid in the soil,
my father dwarfed beside them,
the real creators
of the swollen stooks blurred in the background.
   Then, the middle of the book, the children,
three of us, in turn, perched uncertainly
on their harness-bent backs,
the horses familiar now,
their names — Dick, Tom, Duke,
memories of the long winter rides to school,
trusting them to find home
through the blizzards,
bearing us all to the end of this time,
to the last page, a tractor,
its metallic brutishness proud under my father.

   There is another picture, somewhere,
my mother did not include it here,
of the last of the horses,
the one I still rode to school
until they vanned us to town;
he is in the wagon,
the wagon hitched to the tractor,
he is going to the stockyards.
My father gave me the thirty dollars, to save.
It was the beginning of my leaving.

Späne

I remember my mother
at home
under the sighing lamp
with its moth-soft mantles
making kindling
the butcher knife sliding
easily, gracefully
into the billets
shaving off long, thin slices
(some so thin they curled)
the sound a cry descending
to the thud of das Messer
on the floor
and the sharp wood smell
falling up from the litter
of Späne
that gathered like enormous
white Schneeflocken
around die Füsse
meiner Mutter . . . .

Perhaps
I am still there
alien among my books
watching, fascinated
the keening knife
slice down
through that white
that white
white
vulnerable
wood

White Lilies

White lilies.
Someone has sent white lilies.
Of course, Easter.
There are three blossoms,
back to back,
huge mouths open.
Their heavy scent
stains the antiseptic air,
crawls along walls,
crouches in corners.
My father does not see.
He lies on his back
behind his open eyes
and waits.
I sleep in the chair
and dream of white lilies.
In the morning
one of the flowers
is crumpled shut,
no longer white.
My father is still alive.
It has something to do
with the lilies,
I remember from my dream,
but I do not trust them;
I water them warily.
They turn their two heads
to the bed
and watch.

Good Friday, 1971

In the stiff hospital bed,
its iron sides raised and insulting,
the mound of your body
lies white-sheeted and still.
I know your eyes are open,
staring at the unblue ceiling,
but I stand at the door,
unable to intrude,
and wonder what images recolour
this pastel room for you,
what remembered sensations
are vying with your pain.

Are you thinking of the homestead,
of the early years,
when you cleared the quarter by hand
and were always hungry
and cold and unyielding;
 or before that,
 of the Old Country,
 when you ran
 barefoot in the Bavarian hills;
or later,
of us,

born in this foreign land
of a foreign woman,
your children,
grown and educated now enough
to scorn farm
and Old Country
    or yesterday,
      when the doctor told you the truth,
      and there was nothing more to say?

Then the nurse comes
and says, "go on in,
he's awake,"
and you turn your head
and see me
and we stare at each other,
strangers, unknowing,
across a distance
as deep
as your dying.

Burial

He was born in April.
And this April
they carried my father
across the brittle field
that for 40 years
had shrugged at his crops
and now made room
for the long black pod
of his coffin.
They, too, were farmers
who covered him with soil
in the old spring ritual,
and they believed in resurrection,
in the germination
of that shrivelled seed
in this uncaring earth
this frozen April.

Moved

The earth begins, already,
to reclaim what once was trees;
rotting logs collapse,
roofs are bending
in a slow ballet,
and everywhere
the green grass fires
lick at lumber.
        Already sold, these acres
will be ploughed next year,
remains of buildings
burned or buried,
and a field of grain,
hungry for the newly-broken soil,
will rise from the forgotten
bones of barns.
        Around the yard
the farm machines,
strangely still this fall,
grow from rubber, tired stems.
Their metal blossoms,
huge and red and rusty,
await their own harvest —
auction.
        And we three — born here,
who grew here,
who climbed the trees
        ran down the river-banks,
        swam in the dugout,
        hid in the hayloft,
        rode horses as rein-free as we —
grown weary of wonder now,
cling to our separate cities,
refusing to repay this farm
for what it was
and what we are.

Auction

Rain.
Machinery and furniture
and all my past
in naked rows
across the yard.
The house, garage, and barns
emptied, plundered,
doorways ripped apart.
Strangers pawing
through boxes
of dishes and books,
prodding the chesterfield
with dirty boots
and muttering "junk."
My mother
brave and alone and uncrying
for the husband just buried,
and the auctioneer crying, "Sold!
for one dollar."

The day of the sale
there was rain
but nothing washed away then
or since.

Widow

The clothes were the hardest to face,
the most personal.
She asked the children, urgently,
if they wanted them.
"No," they said, misjudging her need,
and repelled by the thought
of wearing his clothes
or disposing of them.
They hung in the closet for months,
the shirts pressing against her dresses,
the pants beside them on the hangers
with a thin tumour of dust.
She would see them every night
as she undressed,
and every morning they were
the first thing she saw,
hanging there, waiting,
each item speaking dumbly to her
of when it was bought
and where it was worn
and why it is worn no more.
And she would turn her head away,
to the cold mate of her pillow,
and weep with that terrible anguish of loss.
But still she could not bear
to take them down.
When the children came home,
they saw them there,
but they could not speak of it to her.
They thought of the day
they would be taking down her clothes,
piling his and hers together,
as perhaps it should be.

Survival

There was never gentleness.
All this romantic bullshit
about growing up on farms.
All I remember
are the pain and death.
When pigs were castrated,
their screams all afternoon
and my father coming in,
the guilty blood all over him.
When calves were dehorned,
their desperate bawling
and my mother saying,
"it doesn't really hurt them."
When I saw kittens smashed
against the barn walls,
and dogs shot
when they were too old
to herd the cattle,
and chickens
with their severed heads
throbbing on the bleeding ground,
and horses shipped
when my father bought a tractor,
and I could bus to school.
I learned a lot about necessity,
that things are functional, or die;
and I was not as ill-equipped
as first I thought
to live in cities.

The Lantern

My sister, I see,
has a new flower-pot.
When I look closer,
I see it is our old barn lantern —
    painted white,
    undented,
    smelling now
    no more of barns,
    no longer fused
    with cow dung
    on its bottom;
    some fragile purple blossoms
    have their roots
    where once the wick,
    sucking kerosene,
    burned a yellow hole
    into the milk-swishing darkness —
I look for a metaphor in this,
some comment on art and life,
at least on drawing-rooms and stables.

But always,
I see only my father,
walking slowly
past the sagging,
the cow-free barn,
listening still
for our cries of *cobos*
and for the first muted bell
in the distant pasture.

Northbound

> *. . . Berwyn, Brownvale, Whitelaw,*
> *Bluesky, Fairview . . . first call.*

There was always something soothing,
something lyrical,
in that last announcement
in the pure-prose bus depot in Edmonton.
I wondered whether the reader
had appreciated the alliterative litany,
that conjunction of calm colours
and calm sounds;
whether, after the harsh syllables of
> Hinton, Vegreville,
> Wabamum, Ponoka,
> Nordegg, and Leduc

that he pronounced all day,
he would welcome midnight
and the final northern destinations
with their tranquil names.

> *. . . Berwyn, Brownvale, Whitelaw,*
> *Bluesky, Fairview . . . final call.*

Around the depot heads would lift
at the familiar chant,
at the familiar names evoking
the un-city images of home,
and we would rise,
a wayward congregation
returning for communion,
and find, with lessening embarrassment
for both our origins and our forsaking them,
our buses
that would travel through the night
and wake us at Peace River,
with Edmonton rubbed from our eyes,
and our Berwyns, Brownvales,
Whitelaws, Blueskys, and Fairviews
fresh and forgiving as
the morning before us.

from *Land of The Peace*
(1980)

Reconstruction

What is left are the chimney bricks,
rising bluntly in the fields
like a stack of bones.

They have, from single bones,
reconstructed dinosaurs,
the shape surrounding through history
the remaining fragment
like memory of water clings to drought.
As we watch,
the house shakes itself slowly into place,
log walls climb
around the old bricks,
assemble themselves into roof.
Through the windows
we can see
parallelograms of sunlight
lying on the floor.
Smoke rising from the chimney
is tautology:
we know already there are people inside,
can see their shadows
move across the windows,
can hear their lives breathing
across the whole country.

Terry

The children running
                   running home
to be the first to tell:
    the tractor rolled over,
    yesterday, yes, after school,
    on the way to the field,
    crushed him, yes.
Eager with disaster,
watching their parents greedily,
knowing that only such news
will make them pause —
    hands for once still
    on the unfinished fences,
    on the axe incomplete over wood —
knowing that only such news
will make them look deeply
            at their children,
see the fields and the farms
make their premature claim,
see their own children
dead under the overturned machines.

Chop

Running the chopper all afternoon,
he was white with the dust,
the thick flour of grain.
He would stand in the yard and call,
Staub mich ab, and, reluctant,
I would take the broom and go outside,
and he would turn his back to me,
tensing for the blows.
But I never struck him hard enough,
something in me shy with shame,
the dust scarcely stirring
under my apologetic blows.
Harder, my mother would call,
impatient, from the house,
coming out at last and doing it herself.
Her blows would rock his body,
landing solidly on shoulders, back and legs,
the dust whitening the air;
And me standing back,
a child, inarticulate,
watching the blows fall
and his body absorb them,
in that fine tension
of their understanding,
that easy balance
of their practical love.

North of Town

The fist of this town opens,
cracking its fingers north
across pine and spruce and muskeg.

    this is the symbol
        falling on the land
    this is the road
        fitting around itself
        the forest

Culverts knuckle under
        its wrinkle-pleated skin;
ditches fall away like dead cells,
        coagulate with old rain.

The road points into the wilderness,
to this final break with metaphor:
        what would be fingertip
        becomes tree,
        the road becomes path,
        the path does not leave
        the incomparable forest

Double Standards (I)

With my father
it was the purple gas incident.
The RCMP appearing
unexpected
in town,
checking our car
and finding purple gas,
and my father protesting
in impeccable shock
he hadn't put it there
— the oldest son, perhaps,
not him — and
the officer, impressed
with his indignation,
letting-him-off-this-time.
And later, my father,
laughing,
telling the story,
and I learn
that he lied,
learn for the first time
about duplicity,
about the relativity
of absolutes.

Double Standards (II)

With my brother
it was the fencer,
the machine
that sent electric current
pulsing through
the barbed wire fences.
It doesn't hurt, he said,
laid my trusting hand
between the barbs,
and the shock thrust itself
up my arm.
I jerked my hand away,
looked dumbly at his laughter,
such betrayal.

And sometime later
I held the paw
of my pet dog
against the wire.
It doesn't hurt, I said,
laughing,
laughing.

Farmland

The west end of the field
was different.
ragged edges of crops
pleating into riverbank.
an admission of boundaries
beyond the symmetry
of section lines.
the soft collision
of field with space.
the slopes coiling and recoiling
in green parabolas
      folding
            to the final collusion
            with river:
                  the conclusion of land
                  the beginning

Capitalism

The first four years
I rode horseback to school,
    most of the other kids
    coming in by then
    some other way,
    in something motorized
    but less reliable.

So there I was
with the only horse at school,
and it had started to become that time
when horses were a novelty
to my tractor-jaded generation,
and I soon realized
I had a good thing here.

At recess I set up my business:
    a penny a pat
    a nickel a ride
    a dime for the whole noon hour.
There were mishaps, of course,
generally minor,
    resulting mostly from the horse
    thinking it was home time
    and heading eagerly off,
but this seemed only to add
to the thrill.

Business was good,
and word got around.
Eventually it reached my parents,
and I was ordered to stop,
which even then seemed contrary
to the free-enterprise ethic
I was learning elsewhere, everywhere.
But I was hardly in position
to oppose this government intervention,
so I closed my barn doors,
burned the books,
and that was that.

I confess
to a certain nostalgia
for that early entrepreneur,
having never since
been so successfully self-employed.

The Strap

I was eight
my first day of school.
At recess I played like the boys,
mean and tough,
delighted with the ease of leadership
my older sister
always held at home.

> *this will teach you*
> *how to get along with people*
>   and the strap burning
> ten times into each palm
> raying along the fingers
> up the arms
> *this will teach you*
> *to play nicely*
>   and the strap burning
> cutting obedience
> into the open personality
> *you might as well learn early*
>   branding the adult
> into the child.

The True North

We are drawing the maple leaf,
we copy it from a book,
it's our national emblem,
when Laura says,
    what is a maple leaf,
and we all giggle,
imagine asking that,
why, we all know, it's —
and teacher says,
    why, it's —
    the maple tree leaf,
and Laura says,
    how come
    I never seen one,
and we all gasp,
crayons cringing
over maple leaves,
but teacher looks —
not mad, something else,
she looks —
out the window,
at the thick hair
of poplar and spruce
braided across the sky,
and she says,
    you're right,
    it doesn't grow here,
and we wait,
there must be something more,
but she only says,
    finish your colouring,
and outside
the wind accuses
the unknown forest.

Metamorphosis

Something is happening
to this girl.

She stands on one leg
on the third block
of her hopscotch game,
lifts herself forward
to the next double squares,
and, as she jumps,
something changes.

Her straight child's body
curls slowly in the air,
the legs that assert themselves
apart on the squares
curve in calf and thigh,
angles become arches;
her arms pumping slowly
to her sides adjust
to a new centre of gravity,
the beginnings of breasts
push at her sweater,
her braids have come undone
and her hair flies loose around her.

Behind her
the schoolhouse blurs,
becomes insubstantial
and meaningless,
and the boys in the playground
move toward her,
something sure and sinister
in their languid circling.

Slowly she picks up the beanbag.
When she straightens,
her face gathers
the bewildered awareness
of the body's betrayal,
the unfamiliar feel
of the child's toy
in her woman's hand.

Pen-Pals

We wrote with all the ardor
of discovery,
boxes of letters
chronicling our adolescence,
fluent confessions
leaping back and forth
in the merciful mail.

And then our meeting.
He asked if I got his last letter.
Yes, I said,
and the conversation
crumbled from there,
both of us sensing with panic
our mistake,
thinking how we later might
discuss it as abstraction
in premeditated prose,
but knowing already
that everything was changed,
that our letters would fold up
into them now
a great emptiness,
a failure
we could never articulate.

It was left, then,
just to make the graceful end:
the reserved notes,
sent further and further apart
until there were none at all,
only the boxes of old letters
we threw away,
like our childhood,
with longing
and with relief.

The City at the End of It

A slow collage of expectation
assuming the white canvas
of my adolescence,
the city at last
lifted before me
like the sun on the dark horizon,
moving past the bus windows
all glow and promise;
my face in the glass superimposed,
city and self
the same portrait

so far before I would see
the painting finished and flawed,
and the city crumpled
like an oily rag
on the rim of the landscape.

Blizzards

It was
    he said
the horizontal snow
that drove her mad
    blowing in thin and endless chains
    across our windows

not pulling itself down
into the reason of the right angle
    but that constant tearing across
eroding the expectation of gravity
    the vertical reassurance
    on the flat landscape

There was only
that white streaming
into the corners of her eyes
across the pointless prairie

Mother With Child

She rocks the jar of cream
in her lap
like a cranky child,
tries to lull it
to some expected form,
as I see myself
rocked so often
on that tired lap.
Finally, late at night,
the cream thickens, clots,
she pours off the buttermilk,
gives me a glass.
Thank God that's done, she says,
and goes to bed.
I watch the pale hill of butter,
wonder if my own
murky childhood's end
met with such relief,
a sudden falling together
into one shape,
no more weary rocking, rocking
late into the night.

My Mother / My Self

Loving the sharp gassy smell
of the new mantles,
I would lean close
as my father pumped up
    and lit the lamp,
and suddenly my hair was on fire,
    a wild corona of flame
    around my head,
and my mother from across the kitchen
instantly there,
beating the flames out
with her hands.

It has become
part of the apocrypha
I carry with me
from age to age,
    that story,
seeming with the years
more allegory than truth,
but leaving me always
the guilty daughter
    safe
in the scarred hands
of her mother.

Four We Knew

This one hemorrhaged to death
by chopping wood
until her tenth child broke
vengefully from her body.

This one, whose husband died,
had a son of nine who,
knowing he was now the man
and to assume his father's place,
stabbed her when she disobeyed.

This one took her life inside herself
and existed empty for a year,
until her body understood
and hanged itself in the barn.

This one was beaten
every Sunday after church,
for the sins of Eve, her husband said,
it says in the Bible.

In rehearsal,
on Saturdays, four girls, fourteen,
in Confirmation Class,
reciting our end of childhood;
taught what it would mean
to be women in the Church:
men obey God,
and women their husbands.

Punishments

I remember most
being locked in the dark cellar,
the musty earth sealing around me,
the rustle of unseen creatures
in the monstrous corners,
my throat and fingers raw
from imploring the deaf door.
When we were older
the discipline was more direct,
always our images of him
the raised hand,
the freshly-cut switch,
the brutal belt.
That we learned to love him
is not, they tell us, surprising.
That we learned to understand
and to forgive
the tortured child in him
perhaps is.

The Last Picture of My Father

In the last picture of my father
he is sitting in his old chair,
his fingers white and unused on his lap,
the smile on his papery face
having nothing to do
with the cancer
scribbling its ugly address
across his skin,
or with the desperate talismans
we piled around him:
    on his left
    the garish Christmas tree,
    presents effusive under it,
    on his right,
    myself, his daughter,
    young and wearing make-up
    and a green dress.
It is only, I have pointed out,
the colour film
that makes our eyes red,
we were all so careful
not to cry.

Dusk

A dark wing
    slitting
the pale belly of sky,
the hawk
    slides
into the west.
A small death
hangs in its claws.

A dangerous evening.

Later,
the bone-white moon
litters the landscape.

Raw Material

One day contained it:
    my mother in the morning
chasing for miles across the fields
a hawk with a chicken
heavy in its claws,
her slapping at it with a broom
until she knocked the chicken
down and safe;
    and in the afternoon my brother,
rifle over his young male shoulder,
carrying home by the ears
the damp brown body
of the rabbit.

A day so rich in implications:
I wait for the connection,
the pulse across the synapse,
but the images seal shut like seeds,
fact impervious to symbol.

Nazis

Nazis, the whispers began,
Nazis, when they gathered
and poured over each other
memory of the Old Country
to wash away the dust
of the cold Canadian fields.
Nazis, the voices said
to their backs in the town,
Nazis, to their children
bewildered at school,
Nazis, until they kept alien
to their farms and afraid.

Such relief for us all,
the end of the war,
the enemy now redefined:
the stooped Ukrainians
pausing over their plows.
Communists, we said.
Communists.

Immigrants

"If Canada is to remain a white man's
country, it can ill afford to be the dump-
ing ground for the scum of Europe."
(*Saturday Night*, 1921)

English a stone in their mouths,
they translated their lives
into the rhetoric of this country,
plowing the old languages
into the deaf soil,
the anglican rhythms of the factories.

And it comes to this:
their children Canadian
and foreigners to them,
their children, proudly unilingual,
ashamed of the outgrown dialects,
and of the fluent labour
of their parents' lives.

The Way He Told It

Such cold,
the horses white with it,
and my wife, dying,
in the sleigh,
forty miles to hospital,
then getting there,
and they wouldn't take her in.
No money, no doctor,
they said.
And Rosenbloom, he was there,
you take this woman in, he yelled,
I'll pay your goddamned money!
So then it was all right,
they would take her in.
He was Jew, Rosenbloom, they said,
but this is what I remember of him.

Collusion

It is the dog in everyone's past,
the one that dies,
the one that returns in the night
with its usher of flies,
its face bloody and blind,
nuzzling our sleep,.
the one that always finds the child
connecting for the first time
the rifle shot
with the absent animal,
connecting forever
the knowledge
with the guilt.

A Lot to Kill

There was always a lot to kill,
the being, reason enough.
Bears springing reborn from the earth,
hawks multiplying even in the rifle shot,
lynx and deer regenerating in the dim forest,
the forest itself darkening forever
                beyond the eye of the axe.
The wilderness limitless,
our killing of it then,
the last without guilt.

Wild Berries

The wild berries on the riverbank
        that swell in the pagan sun
        seduced by a tawny season
        sucking its blossoms to berries
        and berries to burning
ripen careless
on this arm of earth

Raspberries darken
to no purpose but the sun's
slide slowly from their cores
        drop
among the leaves
like unused words

Blueberries
strawberries
tug anarchic from the soil
    stipple the grass
globe into anagrams
    coded messages
     keyed to perception

Saskatoons sleeving their branches
    in wet clusters
contain also the dead raisin
        the completed stone
are yet at this moment
accessible as a syllogism
      as the hand reaching.

Energy

One of the jobs
was putting up ice in winter,
cutting the big blocks from the dugout,
hauling them to the icehouse.
And then, that miraculous discovery
in burning July,
of the cold still crystallized
in the sawdust,
and me asking my father
why we couldn't save
pieces of heat from summer
the same way.
Him waving at the woodpile
he was building,
saying, there it is,
and it was one of those
epiphanies of childhood,
one of life's great harmonies understood,
and our place in it.

The Farmers' Union

It was poverty
forced the first co-operation,
    the threshing crews
    the wood-cutting teams
    the machines jointly-owned,
pushed them,
    overalled immigrants
    educated by injustice,
    to the picket lines in '47,
and led the co-op movement,
    the twine that bound them
    simple and profound
    as bundles of grain.

They shake their heads
about their children.
Having enough to eat
makes them careless, they say.
Around them family farms
become hungry corporations,
elevators marked Co-op become Cargill,
no one bothers with binders any more,
or threshing crews,
or binder twine.

Pig

They say you make a good pet.
    (I have seen you taken for walks
    on a leash in a Major American City
    with a red bow around your neck.)
They say you are more intelligent than dogs.
    (Yes — dogs have the I.Q. of Q-tips.)
They say you are a good watchpig.
    (I imagine you crouching wary
    at night in my living room
    baring your teeth.)
They say beauty is in a pig's eye.

There is no doubt
your image has changed.

Someday I will sit in my senile city chair
and tell stories to your descendants
sitting on their bored haunches at my feet
    of the barbaric days
when you were bred for food
like the first Pekinese,
    of unjust epithets
like "wallowing" and "filthy"
ascribed to you,
    of you anarchic through fences
plundering gardens
and galloping gracelessly down country roads,
    of all those unenlightened days
when we were simply farmers
and you were simply swine.

Cow

Sometime becomes a precedent,
a referent.
For example.
The child, milking the cow.
The child has learned
the slow, stroking preliminaries,
the bonding of milker and cow
before she lets down her milk.
The child pulls it into the pail
in an easy, tinny rhythm.
   — the cats in a careful semi-circle
   gulping greedy at the stream
   that shatters in their faces —
The pail fills,
settles heavy on the heels of the child,
head against the warm flank,
almost asleep
   — the smell of the frothy milk,
         the cow,
           the hay-hung barn —
And some infant philosophy drifts past,

something about being happy,
about doing a job quietly and well —
      And then:
suddenly, the rear foot has lifted, kicked,
    the milk stool topples
    the child clutches at pail
              at cow
              at air
    everything is flying
    milk-covered cats are streaking away —
And the child is sitting
in a pool of muck and milk,
staring at the cow
with her foot in the pail.

This is the precedent,
the sequence indelible.
And the adult wary
at every complacency,
remembering the cow
with her foot in the pail.

Landscape

It has become
the Abandoned Farmhouse Genre.
In the upper right
is always the grey house
decaying into the ground
and surrounded
by much artistic space.
Sometimes a rusting plow
appears to the left of the house,
and a few rotted fence posts lean
listless in the foreground.
There are seldom trees,
and they never have leaves.
The colours are always dark, dull,
but the rigid line of the horizon
must somewhere bisect the scene.

Yet,
in even the most sentimental of these,
if we look closely,
closely,
we can see the dead farm is real,
a vestigial memory
softening behind the brittle paint,
a real loss,
an unmanipulated sorrow.

Stone

There is something in stones
that blisters them annually up
from the earth
against the logic of gravity,
that grows them like calluses
on the palms of spring fields.

Like the first sea creatures
compelled to the blue air, the sun,
they squeeze themselves to the surface,
shoulder their way
through the passive soil,
and hold their grey and enigmatic faces
to the light:
an assertion of rock,
fragments of an old message
we will collect and haul away.

Farm Women

to Irene Murdoch

You labour for years
in the cold fields of this country,
in the hot kitchens of your houses,
in the birthing of unwanted children

        (you do what you must there is
        no other choice you
        survive)

to this final appraisal
in a man's court of law:
your easeless years
rewarded with a feudal wage,
    your room and board;
your work betrayed as
    just a normal contribution for a wife.

And you sit
with your large-knuckled hands
crumpled on your laps,
beyond even anger
as you see the empty harvests of your lives,
your plantings doomed from the start
by the dry injustice
of these judgements:
        your work worthless,
        the farms theirs.

Picture of the Widow

In this photograph
she stands as she stood
for three weeks after,
silent on the shore,
watching the boneless fingers
of the river
plaiting his death
into her eyes.

    for some sign,
    something to surface,
    an oar to wash ashore,
    anything.

    perhaps trying to learn
    that efficient energy
    of indifference.

    or the other,
    the answer accessible
    in her own obedient body,
    feeling already
    the cold astonishing her feet,
    the pull of current
    at her thighs
    like a reunion,
    everything abstracted
    resuming perspective,
    a final focussing in
    before the shutter
    blinks shut.

Mosquitoes

When the winter liquifies at last,
runs wet fingers
through the roots of fields
leaks into dams and dugouts and sloughs,
tadpoles already darken the waters
like an armada.
There is little time for truce
between the adamant seasons,
before the summer sags with insects,
our skins tear like gauze
beneath their procreative purpose.
The heavy air coagulates
with their survival.

Schools

It is an understandable indulgence
(you have all done this),
a conscious wading in nostalgia.

You stand outside the old school,
you let the memories tide over you,
you walk up the stairs, down the hallway,
you let the memories tide over you,
you stop outside the last classroom.

Look in (the memories tide over you),
it is all still the same,
time has scarcely rippled this place,
the students, you almost remember the faces,
the same desks (the memories),
the teacher is the same,
the lesson the same (tide over you).

You want to rush in,
to tell them . . .
something important,
to give them answers
the teacher has no questions for,
to shout, *this is what life is, this!*

You do not, of course, go in,
and they bend their faces,
familiar yet not, to work,
and you walk away.
What have you learned, after all,
that they would need to know?

Horsepower

Once,
    horses knew poverty.
Once,
    horses bowed their heads shamefully
    into their collars,
    grateful for the blinders
    that hid their eyes
    from the pompous pity
    of neighbours
    with new tractors.
Once,
    horses were humiliated
    by the swaggering machines.

But the horse has made a comeback!
There is a revival of the horse!
Horses have right-of-way at intersections!
Horses can intimidate imported cars
and stare down two-ton trucks.
Horses have become sophisticated;
they trot haughtily around suburban paddocks
and are obligatory ornaments for acreages.
Horses know that every hobby farmer needs them
or would be sneered back to the inner city.

Horses have found a new sense of worth;
a horse is everyone's idea of success.
Is it any wonder
        horses are becoming snobs?
Can you blame them
        for being embarrassed
        at their working-class origins?
Wouldn't *you* try to cover up
        that bastard country Clydesdale
        in your family tree?
Horses have as much right to be bourgeois as we do;
their parents worked hard to give them the good life.
Remember that
        the next time
        one bullies you off the road
        on your way to work
        on his way home
        from a party.

Cat and Mouse

He lies before it
like a voluptuary,
licking his fur.
The mouse moves,
he is on it,
shakes it in his mouth,
bats it with his paw,
but will not kill it,
lets it loose and terrified
to cower in its corner.
I know that I should kill
the mouse in mercy,
even raise the billet above it
like an absolution
    remember the hayfields
    of childhood
    the last mound lifted
    and my pitchfork
    clattering down
    on the scattering mice
    without this adult fear
    of creating death
I cannot.
I lower the billet in shame,
wonder which of us
most civilized.

Arrowheads

For years we collected arrowheads,
the flints like dark tongues
mute under our plows and shovels.
Incomplete legends
clenched into centuries of silence,
they persist
in this forgetful land
    (homestead land:
    we are the owners,
    we are the settlers,
    we are the first).
They persist,
and us only inheritors
of a people
that buried its blood
under our thick crops.

    At the museum, at last,
    they kept only a few.
    A dime a dozen, they said.
The memories so cheap, eventually,
and all of us harvesting still
that history.

Remembering It

the facts:
  that I was driving home
    through the reserve
    and there were three of them
    on the roadside
  that one was carrying
    a bottle by the neck
    like a dead bird
    and threw it
    at a rock on the road
  that the other two, laughing,
    grabbed him
    and threw him
    in front of my car
  that I swerved,
    the car sheered into the ditch,
    the soft thud of hitting him,
    and then that clean accidental silence.

and how it changed:

  i.   he stumbles from under my bumper,
       grins at me,
       staggers down the road with his friends
       past the bottle become shards on the road

  ii.   *you stupid bastards*, I shout,
       watching them go.
       I could have been killed, I think,
       they could have damned well killed me

  iii. when they have gone,
       three fenceposts leaning across a field,
       I get out of the car,
       examine the fender for damage

Harvest

I listen to the pioneers
in their tiny retirement houses in town,
rooms thick
with old furniture and photographs.
One shelf or bureau blooms
with pictures of distant grandchildren,
but there is little else of the present here;
even the clocks chiming the hour
sound years behind.

They show me their albums,
ripe with harvests
    themselves young
        in fields of chest-high wheat,
    the threshing crews,
    new barns and new children
        inheriting the land behind them
        still full with forest.

They tell me of the good-old-days,
and then they laugh,
waving at the walls folding them in,
and say,
    we never had it so good,
    running water and electricity,
    such miracles!
and of course it is true,
of course
it is true.

Men, Snoring

He could awe us all, my father,
with his barbarous snores,
that warfare in his throat
that fired his breath
in staccato volleys
across the room at us,
plundering our evenings.
How do you sleep? I asked my mother,
who could wake to a whisper.
I don't hear it, she said,
which I did not believe,
and filed in memory
under Mother's Martyrdom.

My own men,
when it came my time,
I chose from their sleep,
the Silent Slumberers,
breath easing gently from them
as they lay curled on their sides;
some, I did allow
a placid dream
to bubble from their open mouths,
and later I would even tolerate
those purring gently in their sleep
like cats.

But this one, the last one —
he saws the proverbial logs
of his sleep
with a chainsaw;
his snores have loosened
plaster on the ceiling,
have homogenized the left-overs
in the refrigerator,
have shattered light bulbs
and frightened plants to death.
How do you sleep? asks my mother.
Quite well, I reply.

Alberta

The country broods about Alberta.
    Alberta no longer knows its place,
    Alberta is boom-town,
    Alberta is suddenly rich.
Edmonton and Calgary gloat
on their skylines,
prosperity fattening overnight
the lean new office buildings.

The north has no new affluence.
The old towns still stumble
    along the roadsides,
their roads still crumble
    into washboard gravel, into dirt.
Among the trees
homesteads sink empty into the earth.
Farmers stand
like archetypes
in their tired fields.

The moneyed murmurs of the southern cities
drift past like rumours of rain.

Elevators

These Quebec villages
gather the countryside
into huge spires,
extorting benediction from the skies.
Houses kneel like supplicants
at their feet.

The churches in the prairie towns
are much more modest,
indistinguishable on the horizon.
The true temples here,
garnering the countryside,
declare themselves more quickly to the eye.
Huge eruptions on the backs of the towns,
they petition the skies
with their blunt heads
and homages of grain.

Reunion

Shopping in the IGA,
she looked like the mother
of the girl I knew,
her familiar features
squeezed into the fleshy face,
the dark hair, defeated with grey,
pulling up from her forehead
in that same startled wave.
You haven't changed, I say,
succumbing stupidly to ritual.
She tells me of her children,
      three furtive mad-eyed creatures
      dropped in the aisles around her
      like bruised vegetables,
of the failed farm,
the small-town disgrace of welfare.
I tell her of the city.
When at last we lapse awkwardly apart,
some obligatory time
for such meetings having passed,
she says suddenly,
don't pity me, you know,
and I only stare at her,
my guilt so manifest
it has no defense,
and we turn away,
into the unimagined lives
neither of us has chosen,
so much to pity in both of us.

These Poems

These poems are homesick.
They keep crawling out
    from under my pen
and running back
    to the north.
They will not be domesticated.
They will not be toilet-trained.
They mess all over the page
with their persistent images
    of farm,
they chew through their ropes
    of urban metaphors
and sneak away whenever they can.
And when there is no way out
they curl up spitefully
    underneath their titles
and starve themselves
    to death.

West

(In the late 1960s, over 1960s, over 100
Toronto residents set out in a covered-
wagon for the Peace River country in
Alberta, where they had heard homestead
land was still available. The expedition
barely made it out of Ontario before the
last of its families dropped out due to
financial ruin or disillusionment.)

We failed, yes.
Our friends smile
behind their guise of sympathy.
They knew we'd never make it.
They fold us back
into our thin apartment buildings,
our jobs at the ends of hallways.

We failed, yes.
Our friends smile.
We were anachronisms,
they say,
inheriting a pastoral need
a century too late.
We cannot argue.
They are right.
You'd just have turned it
into city, they insist.
Perhaps, we say,
looking across the taut streets
strung like barbed wire
below us.

But daily the dream
pulls itself across our lives,
soft and unexpected
as cobwebs on our faces.
It nudges our sleep
into the open land,
the acres lying like a revelation
before us,
green and unpeopled.

Land of the Peace

Unrolling out of the mountains
at Chetwynd,
the land reveals itself
like an alphabet,
the characters thrusting up yellow
in chapters of rapeseed and wheat.

I pronounce the names of this place
carefully,
waiting for the dialect
to assert itself
over the language
of city and mountain and ocean.
But the syllables resist,
the words do not remember me;
my voice is the sound
of the stranger.

Mechanics

It is the car's perceptions now
that label the journey.
    The hardtop at last grates into gravel,
        the dust clouds opaquing the road,
    gravel foams into dirt,
    dirt becomes two rutted tracks,
    the declarative grass
        lisps between the wheels.

And the house at the end of it,
    framed in the spattered windshield
    like a smudged painting,
leans empty into the ground.

I wait for whatever it is
I came here for
to find me,
but the car idles uneasily under me.
I am too far in my future
to remember alternatives,
    the bare feet
    in the warm dirt;
the car threatening to stall
chooses my direction.
I back up,
    turn around.

The tires wind up the thread of my coming,
pushing quickly through the mazes of dust
to the smooth clairvoyance of pavement.

Geological Time

When you enter this house
you become an archaeologist,
cautiously peeling away strata
of wallpaper, linoleum, paint, wood,
each new, old pattern
throbbing into years of memories,
more and more clouded
until you are not sure
whether you have passed beyond
your own birth in this place,
to inherited knowledge,
some collective unconscious
lathered like mortar
between the final logs.

You find the artifacts,
predictable derelicts of evolution,
the cracked washbasin, the rusted flatiron,
the brittle calendar with elliptical memos:
May 10: fescue, November 24: Eaton's order.
Pencil lines climb
up a mottled doorframe,
was it you who stood there,
and who measured your growth,
marks like hieroglyphics
you almost understand?

You need the beginnings,
the first excavation,
the root cellar
down the crumbling steps,
into the primal dark,
a few jars of preserves
far back on the earth shelves,
vegetables like soft fossils
ambiguous in their bins,
nothing you can use,
nothing in all these pieces
that defines you
beyond a random genesis
ricocheting across history,
nothing to tell you finally
where you are from,
why you changed,
what you have become.

South

Driving south from childhood,
remembrance banked at the roadsides
       like snow,
blowing in threads
    across my vision;
it tries to sew shut the road,
   but the wipers run
   their skeletal fingers
   through the easy weave;
everything is memory and white,
I move in white stasis
   south
     south
      (the snow dampens)
       south
       (melts)
south to another season
   twenty years away;
the grass at the sides of these roads
has never been young.

New Poems

Murders

Those who came from miles away,
the tourists,
asking which house,
one of them saying,
were there bloodstains.
But ourselves, too,
more disturbingly, ourselves,
walking slowly through the yard
looking for
not really souvenirs
        (a washcloth left
          pegged to the clothesline,
        an old saucepan
        impacted in the dirt)
but some clue,
looking for why this house
too much like our own,
looking less for
why it happened here,
to them,
than why it has not
happened to us.

Farming

Something women learned,
from digging in the dirt,
the wet soil curdling
in their hands,
the first revulsion
of beetles and worms
becoming a slow citizenship
of earth impacted
into their pores.

Something they learned,
    before the gardens fell
    from their fingers
    into imported rows,
from the underworld of weeds:
those like the thistle
who put up a thorny front
but whose roots barely resisted.
those anchored deep
like the dandelion
who surrendered their green maturity
at the last minute
for the root tips
clenched around rock.

and the grass,
the great plurality of grass,
its lateral roots
peeling the earth up
in long strips
of connective tissue
which continued forever,
a network of cells,
the skin of the whole planet.

Something women learned,
digging among roots:
    kinds of survival,
    the possibility
    of living here.

Perspective

My mother in the hayrack
pitching the hay up
into the black box of the loft
where my father's pitchfork took it,
tossed it to the back;
a synchronism asserting itself
through the dry slither of hay,
the pivot of her fork, his fork,
the fulcrum of arm and necessity

until my father's voice — never hers —
saying, *time for a rest*,
and why should I still need to know
if it was because he tired first
or if it was not her right to choose?
And tugging up lately in myself,
like fresh forksful of hay,
a third possibility,
that she refused to give in first,
and a fourth,
that he knew this
and stopped for her sake —
unnerving me
with the increasing complexities
of their lives.

Mutations

"You know these farmers,
they buy this stuff
but don't read the instructions,
think chemicals
are safe like dirt,
mix it with their
bare hands, for chrissake —"

And I listen.
Yes, my silence agrees,
farmers are dumb.
    the unnatural air of the granary,
    my father with his arms
    in the cancerous wheat,
    anything for a better crop,
    a better life for the kids.
    what other instructions
    were there.

University

"He's got a scholarship . . . . Mr. Gates,
your son's up into the middle-class now,
and you won't be speaking the same
language. You know that, don't you?"
Lessing, *The Golden Notebook*

Education an amulet
against the lives of our parents,
it seals our skins against the touch
of old rituals, presses us
into the corners of family gatherings,
fills our mouths with lumps
of harmless reminiscence.

You are different, they say,
you are changed,
too good for us now, they laugh,
needing our clumsy contradiction,
when we should say,
yes, it is all true,
our tongues unlearn daily
the vocabulary of crops and cattle,
there is less and less here
we can explain.

A head of barley:
what has it to do
with quadratic equations,
with medieval literature?
The day we left
we began to believe it,
and now our knowledge fits our hands
like a manicure
too expensive to soil
with the fact of these farms.
Yes, we should say,
it is all true,
we are no longer your children.

They will watch us leave them
and be afraid,
something they wished for
gone wrong,
like a crop so heavy
it lies down in the field.
That it is no easier for us
is the first
of our educated lies.

Suicides

Not the reasons or the means
or even that it seemed
so often, but how
our parents spoke of it,
their voices afraid,
the way they looked
beyond each other, out
at the dangerous fields, and us
storing it carefully,
as children do,
with the accidents,
burning houses, war,
things that
happen.

Translations

and him saying
the man's the boss
because
that's the way it is
and her
mute before such invocations
crying later
in her weary kitchen

the memory
rising around my tongue
like an old idiom
and I fluent too late
and in a new language

Farmhouse

has ripped at the seams,
pulled apart
 stitches of notched logs,
 wooden threads of frame and roof,
the fabric finally rotted through,
exposing, after sixty years,
what it covered to the sky.
Not much to see, the moon must think,
 floorboards turned to grass,
  nests of small animals and insects,
 a simple cube of space,
nothing human left.

Mapping

To walk around the fence:
it seemed a chore like any other,
one he would not delegate
because he trusted no one else.

Only when one day
he brought back a willow branch
that had fallen on the wire
and grounded the fencer,
as though he needed proof,
did we suspect it was different:
some private measure,
a pacing out of property,
inexcusable
in a life that allowed
no such waste of time.

Raining

It is raining here,
sleek, straight rain
that rolls the dust down the leaves,
that twitches the wheat stalks
in the field before the house.
I imagine the cats, their
wary eyes under the steps.
My father stands in the doorway,
holding the screendoor open
with one hand.
Drops of rain hit his face.
There is no other sound.

It is raining here now.
I hear it flutter on the roof,
see it curl around the apples
on the tree outside my window.
My father holds the screendoor open
with one hand.

Doppelgänger

Always there the pale twin
who moves before me,
a guide
in the empty house.
She is the one who stayed,
who married in high school
and kept the farm,
who fills the cellar with preserves,
who papers the walls,
who has children.
If I turn my head suddenly
at the glassless window
I can glimpse her outside,
filling her apron with eggs
or carrying the milk pails
to the barn.
She is stouter than I am,
her hair is shorter,
but I know who she is,
she lives here,
she did not leave.

Old Stuff

All that old stuff, she says,
when every year I rummage
through boxes of photographs,
letters, diaries, mementoes.
All that hardship, she sighs,
her hand touching the pile,
the old soothing gesture.
We drive out to the homestead;
I sniff through the dead buildings
like some blind dog
trailing its vision.
Best to forget, she says,
noting how the careful fences
have folded themselves in.

Later I always know she is right,
imagine my own children
become scavengers of my life.

What the Meek Shall

Her voice so
timid in our kitchen, accepting
the husband who beat her
when the crops were bad,
the rains wouldn't come
    (it was worst the summer just
    before I had the baby, I would
    curl myself around my stomach,
    I guess he was afraid, another
    mouth to feed)
the son who by age of twelve
would demand she warm his meal again
when he came late to breakfast,
would sneer, *it's your job*
    (one day I found his highchair
    in the attic, I knelt in front
    of it, isn't that silly, put
    my arms around it and cried)
her small words falling around us
at the kitchen table, fine
as dust from the fields, as hard
to sweep away

Hasn't she changed, we say,
seeing her in the nursing home
raging down the halls,
you'll see, she shouts into
one of the rooms, *go
away*, hitting at the nurses
who come to get her.
Watching TV in the afternoons,
her fingers stabbing the
arms of the chair, she whispers
furiously into the soap-opera faces
my turn, my turn, my turn

Hotel Dieu

I have come here with his wife.
He does not know either of us.
He looks at us carefully, sighs, shakes his head.
I'm not the man I used to be, he says.
This lucidity disturbs me more than his forgetting us.
I walk the corridors of this unhappy house,
read the familiar names on the doors.
A man plucks at my coat,
his fingers thick and white and confused.
I remember those blue eyes,
but not in that face, not in that face.
Clouds, he says. *Clouds*, like an aphorism.
The nurse comes and takes him. *Sorry*, she says.

These are the settlers,
their large lives crumpled into this place.
Behind their dim rooms lie the homesteads
they cleared from the forests,
their memories whole there,
articulate in yellow fields of wheat.

A woman is crying in one of the rooms,
dry, weary sobs that knead my lungs.
I will not look at the name on the half-open door.
I will not remember her here.

Nostalgia

"Nostalgia denies the home you had, and
promises you a retrospective address in a
better part of town." Scott Macrae

Especially the summers,
you go back
and all that sweet air
and quiet,
the city something
you never became.
You remember your life
opaquing into adolescence,
and you think everything
was possible then
not because you were young
but because you were here;
you forget how the city
yowled like need in your stomach,
how getting out
filled your hands
like rocks you had to throw.
And now you stand,
your choices thick in your veins,
on the old verandah, watching
wind in the pliant grain,
and all you want
is never to have left.

Driving Back

Static on the radio
scribbles out the urban symphony.
My fingers remember
the local frequencies,
country-and-western fills up
the car like a new passenger.
It is a longer drive each time,
the landscape of this place
slowly sticking to the windows,
the rear-view mirror.

> I come as always
> with half-empty suitcase,
> still looking for something
> to pack back to the city,
> never want to take it all
> and be finished

But the land forgets us easily.
My family only borrowed everything here,
the earth pulls it all back
into itself.
Fifty years are just words
we took with us when we left.
We carved our name
into a tree trunk by the house,
into one tombstone,
but nothing that will not grow over,
nothing that the land
did not expect.

> I fill my suitcase.
> stones, roots, a white scroll
> of birch

Reading

The one you needed to do,
in the old home town,
those you were young with
would be there and say, *well done!*
and you finally do it,
and none of them come,
none,
just some of the new ones
who are nice but don't matter

A kind of necessary pain,
like the cramp in your leg,
it hurts most
when you get up,
walk it away.

Sister

She is holding my hand
but I can't remember it,
whether it was something automatic
like smiling for the camera
or whether our mother had to say
take her hand, come on.
Mostly we remember
who hit who first,
who was pushed off the sled,
who tattled to father,
all that stale history still
squashed between us 30 years later.
It becomes easier every year
to think it is too late,
we are too different now,
the letter at Christmas as much
as there will ever be.
But still I return to the old albums,
touch the glassy photographs
with their secrets sealed in.
My fingertips find the two small faces
I want to forgive, find
the sister holding my hand.

The Reader's Digest

Twenty years' worth in boxes under the bed,
there may be more in the basement, we
are afraid to look. *You never know*
when there's something there a person
can use, she says, and this is true.
They are encyclopedias of sound advice,
and edited into easy portions,
the bones all removed from the meat,
and nothing too tough to chew:
how God gave me hope after my daughter
died, how I survived in the wilderness
for three months, I am Joe's liver,
what teenagers want to know about sex,
humour in uniform, it pays
to increase your word power.
And you read them when you're home,
she adds, the clever woman, and this
also is true. The old ones are the best,
the way they smell brown like the earth.
I dig them up like potatoes
from their boxes, pile my lap full.
Curled into my father's old armchair,
I begin to peel back the pages, I am
safe again and home, my mother
hums in the kitchen. Today
we are the people at the end of the stories.

All

All he would have to say is,
remember the time I came home
with a beard and Dad didn't know me,
and we would all laugh,
Mom would say, just by your voice,
I knew your voice, and my sister
would say, the dog kept barking, and
I would say, that was the
summer I got a camera.
It pulls around us
like a drawstring, that time,
when we come together,
awkward and older,
our frayed conversations
trying to thread some memory
of each other,
one of us will only have to say,
remember the time you came home
from the bush with your beard,
and we are all easy again
with each other,
someone will say how
Mom knew his voice, someone
will remember how the dog barked, I
will remember my new camera,
and we are a family again,
laughing on the front porch.